Blindspots:

Everything you
DIDN'T
know you needed to know about
starting your mental health
practice

By

Deirdre Haynes, Ed.S, LPCS, DCC, NCC, NBCT

Chapters

Introduction

Have you often pondered the thought of becoming a private therapist? Do you have a bachelor's degree and don't know what's needed to become a private therapist? Are you already licensed, but unsure of what has to occur to open your own business? If so, you have selected the perfect book to guide you step-by-step to full licensure and create the private therapy practice of your dreams!

After I obtained my masters and education specialist degrees in School Counseling, I contemplated the idea of opening my own private practice. While in school, a professor instructed us to take the necessary courses needed for licensure while the information was still fresh in our minds. Even though I had no intention of starting my own practice, I am so glad I took those classes because when I was ready to open my practice there were no obstacles or hoops to jump through to begin the process.

Once I began the process of becoming a Licensed Professional Counselor, I often wondered what the steps were that I needed to take to open my private practice. I had no real guidance in this area. As you will learn, many are not so forthcoming with information about how they created and established their private practice. However, I believe that information is meant to be shared.

I wrote this book in order to help those that are seeking full licensure as a mental health therapist and for those that plan to open their very own private practice. The road to full licensure and sole proprietorship is not an easy one, but it is definitely attainable.

Follow the seven steps discussed in this book and you will be well on your way to becoming a successful mental health therapist with the added benefit of becoming an entrepreneur in the process!

Are you excited? I am! So let's begin.

Deirdre

Step 1:

Qualifications

"Start where you are.

Use what you have.

Do what you can."

Arthur Ashe

Counselor or Therapist: What's the difference?

Counselors and therapists are terms that are often used interchangeably. They are very similar, but there some distinct differences.

Counselors are Master's level professionals that are not licensed. The degree concentration may vary such as Pastoral Counseling, School Counseling or Family and Marriage Counseling. These individuals are able to work for agencies and schools and provide basic counseling services.

Therapists are licensed by the state in which they reside. They offer clinical counseling services and are also able to diagnose disorders, create treatment plans, and are considered to be medical providers by most insurance companies and employee assistance programs.

Think of the difference in terms of a general physician versus a surgeon. They are both doctors, but one is more specialized.

Education Requirements

The very first step to becoming a fully licensed mental health counselor is to obtain a master's degree in counseling or social work. Social workers follow almost the exact path that counselors do in order to become licensed, but for the purposes of this book I will focus only on the requirements for counselors.

There are tons of schools that offer counseling programs, but not all schools are alike. The school that you need to attend in order to become a fully licensed therapist must be accredited and preferably a CACREP approved institution. It is not mandatory to come from a CACREP approved institution, but in recent years Tricare, an insurance company that caters to military personnel and their families, has <u>required</u> that all of their approved mental health therapists meet the standards of a CACREP institution. Many, many therapists that were seeing clients for years were suddenly excluded. This did not go over well, but Tricare held firm and those therapists either went back to school to obtain needed hours and/or classes or they had to pass the National Clinical Mental Health Counseling Exam (NCMHCE) in order to become an approved provider.

According to the SC Labor and Licensing Board, *"By law, all applicants must have a 48 hour master's degree or higher in counseling or in a related discipline, and the applicant must demonstrate on graduate transcript successful completion of one (1) three-hour graduate level course in each of the following ten areas and completion of a 150 hour counseling practicum:"*

1. Human Growth and Development
2. Social and Cultural Foundations
3. The Helping Relationship*
4. Group Dynamics, Processing, and Counseling
5. Lifestyle and Career Development
6. Appraisal of Individuals
7. Research and Evaluation
8. Professional Orientation
9. Psychopathology
10. Diagnostics of Psychopathology

If you are currently in a Master's level program or if you have already graduated, please make sure that you have taken all of these classes and that you have completed your 150 hour practicum prior to applying. The application fees are expensive and I would hate for you to waste your money because your application will not be approved.

Labor and Licensing Board & The CCE

Once you have obtained your Master's in Counseling, you are now ready to pursue licensure. The first step to licensure is to visit your local Labor and Licensing Board to get detailed information as to the proper steps to follow. This is the same place that hair stylists, barbers, and architects start in order to obtain their licensure.

In South Carolina, the Labor and Licensing Board directs us to the Center for Credentialing and Education, Inc. to obtain an application. The application usually includes a fee ranging from $150-$250 depending on your state requirements. The information requested will range from your college transcripts to course descriptions to your plans for supervision. Please note that a Licensed Professional Counselor Supervisor must sign off on your application BEFORE you submit it to the Licensing Board. This lets them know that if you are approved, you have a person on standby to act as your internship supervisor.

If your application is approved, you will receive notice that you can now sign-up to take the National Counselor Exam (NCE) or the National

Clinical Mental Health Counseling Examination (NCMHCE). You will be directed to the National Board for Certified Counselors (NBCC) to register for your test. Currently the fee is $275 to take either the NCE or NCMHCE.

When I took the NCE there were no study guides available. Candidates studied prior notes taken in class or many chose to use the Encyclopedia of Counseling, written by Howard Rosenthal. Now, there is a plethora of resources and classes available through the NBCC website as well as private therapists that teach courses. If you are interested in purchasing my online NCE Test Prep course, please visit my website at www.dhaynestherapy.com.

The basic set-up of the test is as follows:

1. The test consists of 200 questions and at least forty of them are experimental and they are not scored.

2. The test may take up to four hours to complete.

3. The eight sections of the test are:

   a. Helping Relationships
   b. Professional Orientation and Ethics
   c. Career and Lifestyle Development
   d. Appraisal
   e. Research and Program Evaluation
   f. Group Work
   g. Human Growth and Development
   h. Social and Cultural Foundation

See the references section for more information.

Once you have taken and passed the NCE or NCMHCE, then you are ready to begin your internship. There are many variations depending on the state, but you will be a Licensed Professional Counselor Intern (LPCI) at this point. In order to receive your LPCI license you must pay the $150 fee (SC).

Now, you can begin working with the supervisor you listed on your application. If that supervisor is no longer available then you can opt to complete your supervision hours with a different supervisor. Most supervisors encourage you to have several Licensed Professional Counselor Supervisors (LPCS) in order to see how various therapists work. For instance, some therapists specialize in trauma, art therapy, play therapy, grief therapy and equine therapy. Working with them may help you figure out your area of interest or future specialty.

The supervision process involves completing 150 hours of supervision with your LPCS. The costs for these sessions vary. Some therapists are very generous because they know that you have quite a few hours to complete. Other therapists charge their hourly rate, which is out of pocket, because they are meeting with you which takes away from them meeting with other clients. So, the cost can range from $10 to $250 per hour depending on the LPCS.

You will have the option of completing 150 individual sessions with your LPCS or you may use 50 of those hours participating in a group. Group sessions tend to be more cost effective and quite interesting since you have different LPCIs from various areas of interest sitting in one group. I tend to offer what I call "marathon group sessions" in which we will plan to meet for up to five (5) hours on a Saturday or Sunday. Some of those sessions are in person, but some can be conducted via video or conference call if you have Distance Credentialed Counselor (DCC) credentials.

Supervision sessions vary depending on the LPCS' area of specialty. A play therapist may facilitate sand tray activities while a trauma therapist may discuss EMDR techniques. The format of the supervision session may vary, but the main requirement is for the supervisee to present current cases. This allows the LPCS to stay informed about your diagnosis, treatment plan, and other pertinent information involving your client. This also allows the supervisee to ask questions and gather ideas about how to handle various situations. The supervision sessions could include, but are not limited to, discussion about your cases, video review, audio review, and note/treatment plan review.

Your supervision hours must be completed within a two-year period. Even if you work with your LPCS and are able to complete all your 150 hours within one year, you will NOT be able to apply for licensure until your two-year supervision period ends. During this time, you are also expected to work with clients to fulfill your 1500 hour supervised clinical experience (direct client contact) requirement. This seems like an awful lot, but when you work with clients on a daily basis the clinical contact hours pass very quickly.

At the end of your two-year supervisory period, your LPCS will sign off on your completion papers. You will need to send in those forms and await the final fee information. Usually you will pay a prorated amount for your first provisional year, but you should pay no more than $150 max to obtain your LPC license. After the first provisional year, you will pay the $150 fee every two years and provide continuing education (CE or CEU) credits, if requested, to show that you are obtaining the required hours throughout the two years. The continuing education classes have to be in person, which can be in an online class, and/or self-paced online. The number of required hours needed varies per state so check with your local labor and licensing board for that information.

Step 2:

Practice

Essentials

Congratulations! You did it! You have completed the application, passed the NCE or NCMHCE, and completed your two year supervision. You are now a proud fully Licensed Professional Counselor. Celebrate because you deserve it!

After all the excitement calms down, the questions start to creep in very quietly. What do I do now? Where do I start? Well, again you are in the right place!

Did you know that as an LPCI you are able to open your own private practice? Many people do not do it because they have to have clients and more importantly, they have to have clients that are willing to pay out-of-pocket since LPCIs are not able to bill insurance yet. Some have opened their practice, lowered their costs and began seeing clients during their internship years. It may have worked for them, but most people are not willing to pay an intern top dollar and they sometimes question their skill level. However, there are some that are willing to take a chance on an intern and they will negotiate the price.

I didn't open my practice until I was fully licensed, but since it takes time to get on insurance panels, I did drastically lower my fee in order to "practice." Charging someone $30 or $40 an hour is better than most jobs, but knowing that you are worth so much more makes it a little difficult. However, the practice and skill-building I acquired during those months were well worth it.

It is said that opening a mental health private practice is one of the easiest businesses to launch and they are right! Honestly, if you have two chairs and some privacy then you are in business! I know that is a little crude, but that is all that is needed to open your practice so don't stress.

Of course, most entrepreneurs take time to really think about how they want to run their business. If you haven't then NOW is the time to start. You have to have a vision for your business. So, while you are completing all of those internship hours, brainstorm and write down your future plans.

Activity Break #1: Take a moment to pull out a notebook or piece of paper and sketch your vision for your business. I'm serious! My office looks almost exactly like my sketch and it really made me think about how I wanted the client to feel once they entered my office. So get started.

You done yet? I'm serious. I'll wait.

Hopefully, you completed this activity because it really helped to solidify the task at hand. I remember standing in my fully furnished office and being absolutely overwhelmed at how my thoughts had manifested right before my eyes.

Types of Practices

When you are creating your business concept, you need to think about whether or not you want to work alone or if you will work with or for someone else. Below are a couple of options:

Sole Proprietorship- A sole proprietorship is owned and operated by one person. The business expenses can be reported on the owner's personal income tax (Form 1040) using a Schedule C form.

Group Practice- A group practice is run by several therapists and is usually listed as a LLC (Limited Liability Corporation). The distribution of ownership within the group may vary but it is usually equally distributed between the therapists. The business is its own entity and has its own taxes that are separate from the therapist's personal taxes.

Independent Contractor- This therapist is licensed but chooses to work for someone else's practice but is not considered part of a group. For instance, if you want to make some extra money after your day job, you can be hired to provide services for a person that has a sole proprietorship. You would create your own schedule within the confines of the business and you will be an employee of that business for the length of time that you work there. Usually there will be a contract drawn up that stipulates your duties and responsibilities as well as termination procedures and payment. The employer will file a 1099-Misc form to document your income if it exceeds $600. Otherwise, the employer will claim it as a business expense for services rendered during that tax year.

Location

Location is very important. It indicates what type of client you want to serve and how accessible or exclusive you plan to be. Confidentiality is important not only during the counseling session, but as the client comes and leaves your office. I chose a location that had other offices in the building so that no one would know which office my client went in once he or she entered the building. I also chose a central area in my city that would allow people from all sides of town to come to my office. Another consideration is transportation. Some clients will drive, but if you opt to accept Medicaid your client may not have a car so other forms of transportation need to pass through your area.

To get your juices flowing concerning the location of your office, ask yourself the following questions:

1. Will my clients have to have a vehicle to see me?
2. What other forms of transportation come through my area?
3. Does the building have stairs? If so, how will disabled clients enter your office? Do you have an alternative site or office that they can use when you counsel them?
4. How safe is the side of town your office is located in?
5. If you see clients at night or after 5 pm, is the area lighted? Do police officers patrol your office building?
6. Is the office in the front or back of the building? If it is night, will you or your clients feel safe entering and leaving the building when everyone else is gone for the day?

Activity Break #2: Pretend you are the client. Think about what you like to see in your doctor's office.

1. Do you like to see state of the art technology, clean, white spaces or more of a homey feel in your doctor's office decor?

2. Do you like spacious areas or cozy, small spaces?

3. Do you feel claustrophobic without windows and several exits?

4. What do you think makes a waiting room inviting?

5. What types of pictures, rugs, tables and table accents appeal to you?

6. What colors do you like and what kind of effect will they have on your client?

7. Do you like coffee, water, snacks, and reading material to be available as you wait?

8. Do you like soothing music and smells? Some clients have told me that my signature scent instantly calms them when they come into the waiting area.

9. Do you think your clients would enjoy water features, to watch TV or use wifi to surf the web while they wait for their appointment?

10. Do you keep motivational quotes or calming pictures hanging where clients can see them?

Keep these things in mind as you decorate your office space. You want your client to learn something about your tastes and personality when they enter your office space prior to meeting you.

Rental Fees

Rental fees vary from building to building. Most rental fees range from $200 for a one-room office to $3000 and above for an office suite. Rent is due monthly and can be deducted as an expense from your income taxes.

You can search for office space to rent from various sources. Craigslist, the newspaper, and many other online resources provide listings that are available to be rented. I think the best search option is to get out and drive around the area that you are interested in opening your practice. Many office rental companies will post their sign outside of the office building. That is how I found my office. Simply call and ask about the square footage and pricing.

Once you have decided on your desired office space, the building owner will provide you with a contract. Usually you sign once and it stays in effect until you decide to leave while other building owners will have you sign a lease yearly.

Furniture

After you have decided on your office location, then it's time to furnish it. As I stated previously, if you have two chairs and some seclusion then you are in business. However, most therapists want to have a soothing and inviting office space that requires a lot more furniture. Look back on

Activity Breaks #1 and #2 to decide on the type of furniture you would like to have in your office.

Any furniture store can provide office essentials such as couches, your "therapist" chair, desks, end tables, and lamps. Office supply stores such as OfficeMax or Staples can provide office essentials such as your desk, chair, file cabinets, and paper products.

Phone Services

Your office will need to have a reliable telephone, fax, and confidential voicemail service. Some therapists opt to use their own cell phone rather than pay for an actual telephone line in-office since it is less expensive than having a business phone line. Using your own cell phone has its benefits and disadvantages.

Advantages of using a cell phone:

- Using your own cell phone can be cost-effective and can be written off on your taxes.

- Even when you are out of office, your clients can reach you in case of an emergency.
- You have one bill instead of two or even three if you have a fax line.

Disadvantages of using a cell phone:

- Clients may think that they have 24/7 access to you because in actuality they do.

- Clients sometimes view their emotional distress as an emergency so once they leave a text or voice message, it is important to make contact with them as soon as possible. An office line with voicemail provides you with the opportunity to direct them to call 911 if it is an emergency.

- Clients may forget about confidentiality and text inappropriate or sensitive information to you.

When choosing whether or not to use a cell phone or a business phone line, you have to do what works best for you. However, if you can afford to have a separate telephone and/or fax line, I highly recommend it. This allows you to symbolically open and close your business at set times.

Some therapists have opted to use the Voice Over Internet Protocol (VoIP) system in which the telephone services are cloud based. Many therapists say that this phone service is much cheaper than traditional phone service, however, it is not as reliable.

Fax Services

You will need reliable fax services in order to send information to and receive information from insurance companies, attorney offices, schools and clients. Your fax machine should be located in a safe, confidential place since your incoming and outcoming fax will have sensitive information on them.

Voicemail Services

You will need to have confidential voicemail services. Clients, hospitals, Employee Assistance Programs, and insurance company referral departments will leave information on your voicemail throughout the day. If you don't have voicemail service with your telephone provider then you can use a phone with answering machine. If you opt to buy a phone that has voicemail answering machine make sure that the volume is muted when you are seeing clients to ensure confidentiality.

Also make sure that you direct clients that are experiencing an emergency to call 911 if they call your office after hours or during your counseling sessions. You may opt to pay for an after-hours answering service but they will also direct the client to call 911 in case of emergency.

Malpractice Insurance

Obtaining malpractice insurance is crucial for new and experienced therapists. Malpractice or Liability insurance protects you in case you are sued by a client which is why LPCIs should definitely have malpractice insurance. However, if the organization that you work for covers you then you may not have to pay for your own personal policy.

Almost all insurance companies and employee assistance programs (EAP) require that you provide your current malpractice insurance information before they will take you on as a new provider.

The most commonly required maximums are $1 million for each claim and $3 million annual aggregate per year. The coverage time period may change based on the policy you purchase. Malpractice insurance ensures that if you are sued, you have more than enough money to handle court costs and attorney fees.

I have personally used Health Providers Service Organization (HPSO) since I have opened my business and I have found their rates to be very reasonable. Contact information is listed in the reference section.

Business License

Once you have decided on your location, decorated your office, obtained malpractice insurance then you need to obtain a business license. The business license lets the city know that you own an office space in their area. This also gives them the right to tax you for using their property.

Most mental health therapists fall under the same city coding as other medical providers, so your business license fee may be a little higher than others that operate businesses in a different category. The business license fee must be paid yearly and you will receive a form to hang in your office. The fee is based on your estimated income from the previous year. Fees can vary from $25 or more based on your income and the location of your office. So, if you work part- time at your business, your yearly fee will be lower than someone who works at their office full- time.

Contact your local tax office for the county that you live in to get more information about which county your business is listed in and how you can pay your fees. Please do not assume your office is in a particular county because you may find that the zoning is different from what you expected. Late payments accrue fees so you need to prepare to pay this fee yearly.

NPI number

An NPI number is your 10-digit National Provider Identification Number. This number is similar to your social security number because it identifies you as a licensed professional counselor. Most insurance agencies and other organizations will ask for your NPI when attempting to identify you.

Obtaining this number is as simple as logging into the NPI website and requesting the number. **Please the reference section for NPI contact information.**

Business Tax ID Number

This number is like a social security number for your business. It allows companies to identify your business when you are requesting information from them.

The tax ID number can be obtained from the Internal Revenue Services (IRS). You can use the Business Tax Identification number to apply for tax exemption at local stores as well as to open accounts with different credit agencies.

Please see the reference section for more information.

Business Forms

For the love of paper! Get ready to work with and create lots of forms. The good thing is most of the forms you need have been created by someone else so there really isn't any need to recreate the wheel. If you are interested in purchasing some of the forms that I used for my business, please visit my website at www.dhaynestherapy.com.

1. **Intake Forms-** Clients need to fill out this form to provide basic information such as their name, address, telephone number and insurance information.

2. **Informed Consent Forms-** This form provides background information to the client about you, how your business operates, and your expectations. This form should be reviewed with the client at start of the first session to make sure that both of you are on the same page.

3. **Diagnostic Evaluations-** This form is pretty lengthy, but it gives the therapist an in-depth look at the client's mental, medical, emotional and familial history. This form also needs to be reviewed or completed at the first or second visit. Some therapists schedule a separate session simply to complete this form since it can take up to an hour and a half to complete it. I opted to create an online version that my clients complete so that it is ready to be reviewed during their visit.

4. **Receipts-** This form sounds easy enough, but you probably would not think of creating one or buying a receipt book until you have a client in front of you. I know that I didn't. Some therapists print out receipts from their online accounting program or from a word/pdf

document while others buy receipt books to keep up with their sessions. I opted to create my receipt in word, but I have copies made at Staples. **DHCS Tip**: I have my receipts made in duplicate so that I have a copy of the receipt. This helps when you have clients back- to- back and you don't have time to document everything. I go back at a later time to reconcile my receipts and complete my billing. If you would like to download a copy of my receipt, please visit my website at www.dhaynestherapy.com.

5. **Release of Information Forms**- Sometimes you need to request information from another provider that sees your client or another provider needs information from you about your client. If you are releasing information then you must get the client to sign your release of information form prior to sending the information. This informs the provider or organization that the client is aware that this information is being sent and gives his or her consent that the information be released. If you are receiving information from another provider or organization then the release of information form must be sent along with the request. It should be signed and dated by the client.

Fees and Payments

As a private mental health therapist, you have the opportunity to create your own fee schedule. Depending on the person, some will run wild with this fact and others will undersell themselves. When you are setting your fees, think of what you bring to the table (i.e. skill sets, degrees, certifications, etc.), client base income levels, and your business upkeep to start. You definitely want to get paid what you are worth, but you don't want to drive up the fee in the name of being greedy. Most therapists charge $90-$250 per hour depending on their level of expertise and their client's ability to pay. If you have rich, cash only clients that are willing to pay $250 for one hour with you then by all means charge them and reap the benefits. However, the vast majority of therapists are primarily insurance-based and this leaves them at the mercy of the insurance company's set rate. Make sure that the fee shows the client that you are worth their time and money, but is fair so that more people can see you.

I personally opted to accept cash as well as insurance plans. I wanted to appeal to middle to high income individuals and couples. Later, I opted to accept Medicaid as well. I believe that all people deserve high quality therapy and I couldn't be happier with my decision.

To make the process easy for clients to understand you need to create a Fee Schedule form. This form will tell them how much you charge for each of your services. My form indicates how much I charge for 30, 45, and 60 minute sessions. It also breaks down how much I charge for the preparation of paperwork for my client that is requested by other agencies like attorney offices, and disability claims offices.. This form should be reviewed as a part of your intake packet in case any of those situations arise during your time working together. Please visit www.dhaynestherapy.com to purchase a download of this form.

Once you have your fee schedule in place, you need to know how you will accept payment. Most clients don't use cash, but some do. So, if they have credit cards what do you do? Square solved this problem for me, but there are several companies that lease their credit card machines for a monthly fee. I chose Square because they only charge when you swipe their card. I started with the small square plug-in on my phone, but eventually I purchased the Square register. It eliminates the use of my phone to process a sale and the larger machinery makes it easier for a client to complete the sale. Square also provides analytics about your sales for the month and year as well as what items sold the most in a given period of time.

I used to accept checks, but after having one or two checks to bounce, I decided to discontinue that practice. If a client's check is returned, contact them to notify them of the returned check and ask them how they plan to pay. Give them a window of time to bring in the check. Most clients will readily redeem the check, however, if they fail to do so then you can take the check to your local Magistrate office and have them collect the funds.

So, you have completed the basic setup of your business. You should be off and running right? Yes, but there is so much more! Let's get going.

Insurance Panels

While you are setting up your physical office, there are a couple things that you need to do to really get your business up and running. One of the main things you need to do is apply to various insurance agencies to see if you can become one of their providers. If you plan to be a cash only business then you can skip this section.

Insurance applications can be very tedious, but once you complete one of them you are prepared to complete them all. Most insurance companies request basic information about your business along with your LPC license information NPI information, Tax Identification information, Malpractice Insurance information and a W-9 form. Some companies are very strict about how you fill out their form and deny it based on missing information which is why it is important to carefully fill out each section. Then check and re-check that all the information they are requesting has been placed in the packet you are about to mail off. I, personally, haven't had any problems getting on insurance panels, even Medicaid or Tricare, because I make sure I check and re-check my packet prior to sending it off. If I have any questions I call them to make sure I understand what they are requesting.

The insurance packet is time-consuming, but it gets easier the more you do it. The wait time to find out if you are a provider is at least six weeks. Some companies move faster, but many have a tedious process to complete prior to approving you.

Once you are approved, they will contact you via mail or via e-mail letting you know what your next steps are and how to set up your profile with their company. At that time, you will be considered to be a provider and listed as a possible contact for their customers.

Insurance companies pay you based on their own fee schedule and not according to your fee schedule. Your pay will be based on your level of education even though some insurance offer a flat fee no matter the level of education you have obtained. So, even if your hourly fee is $100 per hour, the insurance company may pay you $77 per hour. Either way, you have the option to accept their fee or to not accept their fee and not become a provider for their company. Medicaid tends to pay your hourly fee up to a certain amount which is why many people opt to become a Medicaid provider. However, that full payment comes with a lot of documentation which turns some people off from accepting Medicaid. The good thing is you have the right to choose what types of insurance you will accept, if any, because it is your business.

Remember that from that time on when you call you are a provider and they will ask for your NPI number or Tax ID number prior to giving out

So, you have completed the basic setup of your business. You should be off and running right? Yes, but there is so much more! Let's get going.

Insurance Panels

While you are setting up your physical office, there are a couple things that you need to do to really get your business up and running. One of the main things you need to do is apply to various insurance agencies to see if you can become one of their providers. If you plan to be a cash only business then you can skip this section.

Insurance applications can be very tedious, but once you complete one of them you are prepared to complete them all. Most insurance companies request basic information about your business along with your LPC license information NPI information, Tax Identification information, Malpractice Insurance information and a W-9 form. Some companies are very strict about how you fill out their form and deny it based on missing information which is why it is important to carefully fill out each section. Then check and re-check that all the information they are requesting has been placed in the packet you are about to mail off. I, personally, haven't had any problems getting on insurance panels, even Medicaid or Tricare, because I make sure I check and re-check my packet prior to sending it off. If I have any questions I call them to make sure I understand what they are requesting.

The insurance packet is time-consuming, but it gets easier the more you do it. The wait time to find out if you are a provider is at least six weeks. Some companies move faster, but many have a tedious process to complete prior to approving you.

Once you are approved, they will contact you via mail or via e-mail letting you know what your next steps are and how to set up your profile with their company. At that time, you will be considered to be a provider and listed as a possible contact for their customers.

Insurance companies pay you based on their own fee schedule and not according to your fee schedule. Your pay will be based on your level of education even though some insurance offer a flat fee no matter the level of education you have obtained. So, even if your hourly fee is $100 per hour, the insurance company may pay you $77 per hour. Either way, you have the option to accept their fee or to not accept their fee and not become a provider for their company. Medicaid tends to pay your hourly fee up to a certain amount which is why many people opt to become a Medicaid provider. However, that full payment comes with a lot of documentation which turns some people off from accepting Medicaid. The good thing is you have the right to choose what types of insurance you will accept, if any, because it is your business.

Remember that from that time on when you call you are a provider and they will ask for your NPI number or Tax ID number prior to giving out any information so make sure that you have that information available when you call.

Please visit www.dhaynestherapy.com for a free listing of national insurance companies.

Employee Assistance Plans

Once you are approved to be on an insurance panel, the employee assistance program for that company may contact you or you may be asked by a client if you are a member of their company's EAP program. Since you have already been approved to be on their insurance panel, getting into their EAP program is much simpler.

The EAP is a separate company that provides a specific number of free visits to your clients' place of employment. For instance, if you work for a local Wal-Mart then they may pay Such and Such EAP to provide mental health and other services to their employees. This is an added benefit for working with this specific corporation.

The corporation will only provide a limited amount of sessions. The most I personally have seen is six sessions that can be renewed once every year. After the six sessions are up then the client can choose to continue to see you and use their insurance company. Some clients will stop sessions with you when they learn they have a co-pay while others will gladly opt to continue to pay out of their pocket. It is all a part of the process.

Sometimes a company will issue a "mandate" that the client must go through the EAP for mental health services. If the client has shown deficiencies on the job, they may decide to require them to seek help in an effort to save their job. If the person does not improve after the required amount of sessions, usually three- to-six sessions, then they may be terminated. Your feedback and notes will be taken into account during the final decision-making period.

EAPs usually pay a set amount that may or may not be your set hourly fee. Once you enter into contract with them you are agreeing to accept the amount that they have offered. In most cases, this is not a negotiable amount.

Additional Essentials to Consider

Business Signs

Purchasing a business sign is not mandatory but it is something to consider once your business is up and growing. Clients often have a hard time finding your office if it is located in an intricate network of offices. So, having a business sign located near the street as well as a business sign indoors really helps your client locate your office faster and it looks professional as well.

Your Office Library

As a therapist, you will probably consult many books and textbooks as you hone your skills and develop your specialty. Creating an office library is also optional but it is a great resource. I recommend purchasing Treatment Planners and Homework Planners to use when you are creating your client's treatment plan and/or reporting treatment goals to insurance, disability or legal companies. It makes your verbiage appear to be more polished and concise.

Also, having books that you can lend or at the least recommend to your clients is a great practice. I often refer to books such as "The Five Love Languages" (Couple/Marriage Counseling), "I Hate You, Don't Leave Me!" (Borderline Personality Disorders), or books that discuss the Inner Child or Trauma. Most will jot the name down and pick the book up themselves, however, I have lent a few books out that were returned upon completion. **Please note that I have created several journal-books based on various mental disorders and within these books I have provided areas for your clients to write down book titles you give them and other discoveries they want to jot down. For more information, please visit my website at www.dhaynestherapy.com.*

Websites

A website is a wonderful way to not only advertise your business but to provide needed information to your clients. After you answer the phone and repeat yourself a couple thousand times, I'm sure you will begin to brainstorm ways to circumvent the spiel that you have to repeat over and over.

A well-rounded website should include some, if not all, of the following information:

1. **<u>Welcome Page</u>**- A welcome page or message that allows the viewer to get a feel of your business. Your logo and pictures of your office may help the viewer feel more comfortable requesting your services.

2. **<u>Profile Page</u>**- Your profile picture and credentialing information page should include detailed information about who you are, your credentials, and your area(s) of specialty.

3. **<u>Services Offered</u>**- You can put what services your business offers on this page as well as the fee schedule for these services. You can also include the insurance panels you are approved for and possibly co-pay information.

4. **<u>Products Page</u>**- A product page is optional. If you have written books or have products that you have created that you would like your clients to purchase, you should create a page that showcases your products.

5. **<u>Contact Page</u>**- You should have a page that provides information to the client about how they can call, fax, or email you. You may also include your address and directions to your business.

These are some of the nuts and bolts pages your website should have but based on your area of specialty you may have many more areas for your clients to visit. Remember, most clients want to learn as much as they can about a possible therapist prior to meeting them. Your website could be an open door your clients can use to decide if they want to work with you or someone else.

I have had clients say they chose me because they liked my logo, they liked my color scheme and maybe their favorite color is blue, they liked that my website looked professional, and some said that they chose me because the website answered most of their questions without them even speaking to me. You will never know why a client decides to work with you and not the other tens of thousands of therapists out there. So, remember that first impressions are important and your website is often the first impression that your client may have of you.

Referral Roster

If you encounter a client that you believe is beyond your level of expertise or who could be better suited by seeing another therapist, you need to have a listing of therapists that you could refer the client to see. This is important because if you are unable to fully serve the client then you are doing the client a disservice. Having a list available would be extremely helpful in making a smooth transition for the client. My recommendation would be to create a list and have that person's area of expertise listed beside their name as well as contact information. If they are a colleague of yours, I personally contact them to let them know that you are referring a client to them.

The referral roster is also important if you decide to close your business temporarily or permanently. A therapist may go out on maternity leave and may ask another therapist to take her clients. The same may occur if you decide to close your practice. Proper etiquette requires you to let your clients know as soon as possible and to provide possible referrals to other therapists. The last thing you want to do is make the therapeutic process painful for a client. Your negligence could be traumatizing to a client.

ADA

The acronym, ADA, stands for the Americans With Disabilities Act. The Americans with Disabilities Act of 1990 (ADA) prohibits discrimination and ensures equal opportunity for persons with disabilities in employment, state and local government services, public accommodations, commercial facilities, and transportation.

This act is important to therapists because it is our obligation to provide services to all clients including the disabled. Now, the accommodations that need to be made are within reason but there needs to be a plan in place in case you get a client that is wheelchair bound. If your office is on the first floor then you have nothing else to do except insure that there is a ramp available to access the sidewalk. If your office is upstairs, things can get a bit more tricky. If the office building has an elevator then you are secure but if it doesn't then you need to have a plan in place to be able to provide services for that client. Therapists can opt to meet the client at home or to rent/borrow a space from another therapist that can be used to serve that client. If your office building has several floors, you may be able to lease a space on the lower level as needed.

Step 3:

Got Clients?

We have discussed many key elements that are needed to create the mental health business you have always wanted. However, we are missing one extremely important element, the client.

Patient versus Client: A Quick Terminology Lesson

Whether you call the person that seeks your services a patient or a client is entirely up to you. However, I wanted to mention some important differences in the terminology.

Patient- "a person receiving or registered to receive medical treatment."

As I stated earlier, insurance panels consider mental health therapists to be medical providers. We are often lumped in the same category as doctors, nurses, dentists, etc because we diagnose, create treatment plans, and work with insurance companies/disability companies just like a medical doctor. We specialize in issues affecting mood, personality, and some biological issues. With that being said, some people have opted to call the people that come to see them patients. Now, most people will not mind this but some will. The reason is that you are not a doctor or psychiatrist. You are a mental health or behavioral health provider. Also, calling someone your patient may invoke a feeling of inferiority within the client instead of a feeling of equality among team members.

Client- "a person or organization using the services of a lawyer or other professional person or company."

Calling the people that come to see you a client seems to be more user friendly to me. It suggests that you provide a service and this person has entered into a contract of sorts with you to obtain help with their issues. In my humble opinion, it suggests that we are on a team working together to help you get back to your effective level of functioning.

Again the choice is yours but choose wisely.

The Ideal Client

When you open your private practice it is important to have in mind your ideal client. This is not to say that you may attract some less than ideal clients, but if you know who your target market is then you are more likely to advertise in places or ways that will attract those ideal clients.

So, who is your ideal client? Do you want a client that is wealthy, middle class, or clients that accept Medicaid? Will your ideal client pay for his or her sessions out of pocket and at your full asking price or are you willing to offer a sliding scale to those that are unable to pay the entire fee? Is your ideal client college educated or the average hard working man or woman that is having an major life issue and needs help?

These questions and so many more need to be answered prior to you accepting your first client. Oftentimes, new private practice owners accept anything that comes in the door in the beginning. This is totally understandable because you have bills to pay and you can't get that accomplished sitting in the office by yourself. However, at some point you need to figure out how to weed out those clients that don't motivate you to be a better therapist while targeting those that do.

One way to do this is to figure out what your area of specialty will be. As therapists, we are trained and qualified to see anybody that walks into our office. However, as I said earlier, that is not always the best system to create the business of your dreams. Figuring out and promoting your area of specialty may take some time, but it is an important part of creating a business you love and attracting your ideal clients.

There are many specialty areas. A few examples are listed below:

Children, Tweens and Teens- Any private therapist can work with children ranging from ages five to eighteen years of age. If you like working with children, then your specialty area may be Play Therapy. Play therapists can work with adults as well, but they generally work with children, tweens, and teens using toys, sand, and other games in order to help them develop coping skills.

Adults- As a private therapist, you may decide to only work with adults. This is the most common age-group that therapists tend to treat. The reasoning is simple. Most adults are the ones that have decided they need help and have searched for a private therapist. Even though you may decide to only work with adults you can still specialize in different areas. Some therapists have opted to become couple/marriage experts, grief experts, LGBTQ experts, Vocational experts, Hoarding experts, or my personal specialty area which is Trauma and PTSD. To become an expert in your field, the therapist will take classes, courses, and obtain certifications based on that specialty area on a yearly basis to obtain their required CE credits for the year.

Geriatrics- Another population that you may choose to work with are populations that are 65 years and older. Many of these clients are facing major life challenges with their health, mourning the loss of family members, or may be facing their own mortality. Some therapists have opted to specialize in Hospice therapy.

Activity Break #3: Take a moment to think about what areas of counseling you enjoy by answering the following questions:

1. Do you like working with kids, teens, women, men, or the elderly?

2. Do you find yourself drawn to people who are dealing with issues related to grief, trauma/PTSD, relationships, marriages, job skills, family issues, spiritual or LGBTQ issues?

3. Do you find yourself enthralled with serious mental health issues such as schizophrenia, dissociative personality disorders, and obsessive compulsive disorders?

Answers to these questions will help you flesh out what is of interest to you. Of course, if you are interested in Trauma and PTSD, as I am, that doesn't mean that you won't treat clients with all the other mental health issues listed above. However, the goal is to have the majority of your clients fall into your ideal client parameter.

I know someone is asking the question, "What if I have more than one area of interest? Can I have more than one specialty?" The answer to that is... you sure can. Your business is your business so if you want more than one area of specialty, then I say go for it. One caveat is that even though some specialties overlap, like marriage, couples, and family counseling, it can be a little tricky when you want to advertise. This is what creative marketing is all about. You need to figure out a way to market all the different areas of expertise. You don't want to confuse your potential clients so make sure that you are clear and concise about your area specialty.

So, how do you get clients? If you are a cash only provider, then clients will come through your advertising campaigns. You can advertise on the radio, TV, in newspapers and magazines as well as via social media and via e-mail. There are a wealth of resources to attract your ideal client.

Obtaining clients through your insurance companies and EAPs is very easy. Once you are a provider, they select you. I chose to go this route and I can honestly say that I have not had an opportunity to advertise! Once a client chooses to come see me then I do my best to keep them on as a client until they are stabilized. Many have stabilized, but sent their friends and family to me so it still washes out.

This is a great spot to say something quick about clients. Most clients will not stay with you for a lifetime. I call it the ebb and flow of counseling. Clients come to you when they feel their life is out of control in some area. You are there to help them become more stabilized and teach them coping skills for when the times get rough again. Once a client feels better, they will usually see you less often. The ebb and flow in my office tends to start at seeing a client once a week. I have had a few instances in which the client wanted to see me twice a week. So, they see me once a week and when things get a little better they may start scheduling themselves every other week. As time passes, they may see me once a month or every three to six months. Some drop off all together. Some drop off for a year or two and then come back feeling somewhat ashamed. I am quick to reassure them that this is EXACTLY how therapy is supposed to work. My favorite thing to tell them is, *"I am supposed to be working myself out of a job."* In other words, if I am doing my job correctly, they should stabilize and not need me as much. It's kind of like watching a baby grow up. At first, they are very needy and fearful, but as they learn that it's okay to experience life and that I'm there if they need me, they are more likely to continue to venture further and further away. Finally, they figure out that they can walk without support. That is my ultimate goal and my proud "momma/therapist" moment! So prepare for your clients to leave and allow that process to happen without judgment.

Another great resource is *Psychology Today.* I have gained many clients from this resource. You pay a monthly fee to be listed as one of the providers on this site. Due to its great SEO setup, when clients type in "counselor" or "therapist" or even your name on the internet, this site tends to pop up. I have a website so some select that option, but either is fine because it points the client in the right direction.

Once the potential client is on Psychology Today, they have the option to browse available therapists. They can filter the therapists based on location, expertise/specialty, accepted insurance, gender, and many other options. It is a great resource and currently the fee is only $29.95 a month.

Keep in mind that word- of- mouth is the absolute best advertisement there is! You want your clients to feel that you helped them and if they see someone they know dealing with some issues, then they will think to refer them to you. That is the ultimate compliment. I have had groups of guy friends, professional athletes, as well as work colleagues continue to refer friends and people that they care about to my practice. Even though I never comment as to whether I know the person who referred them to me or not, I often say, "Oh, ok…" and then continue with my spiel about being happy to meet them and other appointment setting information. This is due to client confidentiality and I protect my clients at all costs.

Step 4:

Before The

Session

Now that you have an interested potential client, how do they schedule an appointment with you?

Most clients will call in to request an appointment with you. Many will ask questions about billing and how the therapy process works. This gives them an opportunity to learn more about you and/or your business. Whether you or your secretary answers the phone, there needs to be a high level of customer service present during the call. Clients need to feel welcome to come to your practice and that you are happy that they selected to call you out of the thousands of available therapists in this field.

Once the client has committed to coming in to see you, then you can use an hourly scheduling book to put the appointment down or a cloud based system to enter in the information.

Online appointment scheduling systems

In the beginning, I wrote my appointments down in my handy dandy day planner and kept it with me at all times. This worked well until I started getting really, really busy and ended up having two clients show up at the same time! This was very uncomfortable, but it worked out.

In an effort to not have this happen again, I decided to purchase an online appointment scheduler program. The online appointment scheduler that I use is SimplePractice. It not only keeps my appointments secure and organized, but the best feature yet is that it allows my clients to book their own appointment. This saves me time and effort when clients are unsure of when they will be able to attend a session. We don't have to go back and forth or play phone tag to set up a mutual time. They simply log-in and they see only the appointments that are available. If it is a month out then they know you are booked up until the next month. This program is so worth the $49 I pay a month! It also allows you to enter your session and psychotherapy notes and maintain your billing but I will go into more detail about that in a later chapter.

I have my SimplePractice account connected to my website so that whenever someone visits my website they are not only able to learn about me and complete required forms but they are able to book appointments with me. I love the convenience this technology brings to my practice!

Client Prep Before Session

Once the appointment has been booked both you and the client have a couple of things to complete.

1. **Intake Form-** This form provides basic demographic and insurance The first thing the client needs to do is to complete the intake forms for your practice. The main forms that you need to create or purchase are as follows:

2. **Informed Consent Form-** This forms outlines the policies, procedures and expectations within your practice.

3. **Diagnostic Evaluation Forms-** You can include this detailed form in your packet to save time. Many therapists schedule an

entire session for up to one hour and thirty minutes to complete the packet. After answering the questions in the packet concerning their medical, mental, emotional, and physical history, you can provide your diagnosis.

4. **Client Rights**- The Client Rights form informs the client about his or her rights within your private practice.

5. **Fee Schedule**- The Fee Schedule is that form I mentioned earlier that lets the client know what you charge for your services. This includes in-session fees as well as the compilation of materials for possible disability claims, legal cases, etc.

6. **HIPAA Notice of Private Practices**- The HIPAA Notice of Privacy Practices is a form that describes how medical information about you may be used and disclosed. Clients have the right to agree with what information can and cannot be sent by their mental health provider.

7. **EAP Intake Forms-** The Employee Assistance Plan intake forms are the required forms that your EAP provider needs completed when you begin seeing one of their referred clients. Usually the client will have forms to complete and you will have to complete and send forms as well.

Once these forms have been completed and submitted to you then your client is ready to start sessions with you. You can opt to have clients submit paper claims to you or create form that can be completed and submitted online. I started out with paper claims but I have sense created forms on my website that can be submitted electronically. This is a convenience that many of my clients have said they enjoy. The online forms tend to be completed more frequently and completely than the paper forms. The completed forms are sent electronically to my secure email. I can store them there or print them out to keep in my in-office client files.

Therapist Preparation Before Session

The therapist has a couple of important things that need to be in place prior to the first session. Taking care of these tasks prior to the session will allow you and the client to be stress free during the actual counseling session.

CoPay

One of the first things you need to do prior to you first session with your client is to figure out if they have a copay or not. This can be done by logging into the insurance portal or by calling the insurance provider and speaking to a customer service representative. They will tell you if the client has a deductible or not. If the client has a deductible, then they will have to pay your fee out of pocket. **DHCS Tip:** If I already know what their payment and copay will be then I usually just charge them that amount. So, if insurance will probably pay $77.23 then that is the charge I will charge instead of the flat fee of $100. That is a courtesy I provide and is not necessarily something you must do.

If they do not have a deductible to meet then they will pay their co-pay and I will bill their insurance company for the remainder. Usually copays range from $20 to $40 for most insurance companies. Many companies do not have a copay and pay the full amount of the session, so it is important to find out this information prior to the session so that you don't overcharge or undercharge the client. Either of those situations is not good business practices and affects your cash flow.

Prior Authorizations

Now that you are on insurance panels, this will one of the first times that you utilize the insurance company's website and/or call the insurance company's provider line. I don't know about you but the first time that I called Blue Cross and Blue Shield and they asked whether or not I was a patient or provider, it really felt good to say I was a provider. I think that is the first time it really dawned on me the importance of the work that I do. Ok, back to the subject at hand.

Please note: Many insurance agencies have a separate area assigned to what they call Behavioral Health providers. So, whether they say Mental Health or Behavioral Health, they are referring to all mental health therapists.

As a provider and entrepreneur, you have to make sure that the client's insurance is active and that you will be compensated for your time. So, it is best to check with the client's insurance carrier prior to the visit. If you are an approved therapist, then you will have access to the client's information online and it is as simple as logging in to check the status of the client's insurance plan. You will be able to quickly see if the plan is Active on Inactive. If it is Inactive, then the client no longer has a policy with that company. You will need to contact the client to find out if they have another insurance policy or plan to pay in cash. **WARNING**: Even though you will get very busy, trust me when I say that it is better to check into the client's insurance policy PRIOR to the session rather than wait, see the client, and then not be compensated because they don't have any insurance or money to pay you. Taking time ahead of the session will give you the opportunity to cancel the appointment if needed. If you are blessed to have a secretary or receptionist that can do this for you then by all means utilize them. If it is just you in your sole proprietorship then you need to make the time to check.

In the past prior authorizations were required in order for you to meet with the client. A prior authorization is basically a notification, verbally or in writing, that lets the insurance company know that you will be working with one of their clients for a specific issue, and possibly for a specific period of time. Nowadays, many insurance companies have started to view mental health therapists as a different type of medical provider. So, just like a client can choose a doctor that want to see as long as they accept their insurance, they are able to select a mental health therapist that accepts their insurance as well.

Some insurance companies allow you to request a prior authorization, if needed, online. However, this can take days to obtain. I have found it more time-efficient to call in and get it on the spot. Be warned that some insurance agencies are more simplified than others. This means that some allow you to all in and simply request sessions for the client while others have you meet with the client and then submit oodles of paperwork to see if you have the remote possibility of being compensated. I know it is crazy, but that is not how most insurance companies and Medicaid work. I'm just warning you about those that do have a lot of red tape to get through in order to compensate you.

Once you have obtained the prior authorization, they will inform you of the number of visits they are approving and provide you with an authorization number. You may need to submit the prior authorization number when you invoice them or you may need the authorization number if you call in to ask a question or attempt to obtain more visits. Either way, keep a Client Profile Sheet in the client's folder that has this information on it as well as more detailed information about the client such as their name, date of birth, client number, address, telephone number and number of visits. If you are interested in purchasing this form, please visit my website at dhaynes@dhaynestherapy.com.

Accepting Payments

Now this is the fun part! You have secured the client and ensured that you are a covered provider for their insurance carrier. Now, you need to figure out how to accept payment for your services rendered. You definitely don't want to meet with the client and after it's over be fumbling around trying to figure out how to accept payment. So this is very important.

Most therapists accept cash, credit cards, debit cards, medical spending cards and checks. I used to accept checks but because I didn't have a scanner that can check to see if the funds are available immediately, I got burned several times. What I mean by burned is that the client's didn't have the money to pay so I was not compensated for services rendered in some cases. Most states have a Magistrate's office that has a Worthless Check division. You simply take the check to them and have them pursue the client (threatening jail time) unless they pay the fee by a given date. If they pay then you can recoup your payment and the NSF fee/chargeback to your account.

With that said, most client's fully intend to pay and they do pay you. If they present you with cash, then you need to give them a receipt for their payment. **DHCS Tip:** I recommend keeping a ledger (online or an actual paper ledger) for all cash payments. I personally write that I received cash, checks, or debit/credit cards on the client's receipt. Once I am ready to complete my billing, I refer to those receipts, and not my memory, to make sure that I have accounted for the cash income that I received. This also helps at tax time. Keeping an orderly record of your cash payments will make it easier for you to account for all the money your received throughout the year.

Business Checking Accounts

If you accept any form of payment you need to have a business checking account set up to put the money in. This keeps your business money separate from your personal money.

Opening up your business account is the same process you used to open up your personal checking account. However, they will require your tax id number so you need to have that prior to attempting to open the account. Different banks will have different fees for business accounts and some banks don't charge any fees to open a business account with them. You need to contact your local bank to find this information.

Chargebacks (fees for returned checks that were deposited to your account are costly and insufficient/overdraft fees are more expensive than what you would incur in your personal account. It is very important to curtail those costs as much as possible so that you will stay in good standing with your bank.

Credit Card Payments

If you are going to accept debit cards or credit cards then you have to have some type of point of sale machine. I have found that the Square system works well for my needs. You have a small square plug-in if you need to accept credit/debit cards on the go. This works great when you are selling products at various locations. Simply attach it to your phone, enter the dollar amount, swipe the card and then have the customer sign. The money will either be held at Square until you request that it be transferred to your account or you have opt for immediate deposit for an additional fee. The fees are relatively minor. You will pay 2.75% for the swiped transactions and 3.5 % plus $.15 for manually entered transactions. If you opt to have your money transferred immediately to your account then they charge an additional 1% fee.

The Square system may seem like it has a lot of fees but if you opt to accept credit cards then the card reader will have to be purchased for a fee and you will still have a transaction fee for them to process the credit/debit card purchases.

Receipts

Prior to seeing the client you need to figure out what type of receipt you will give to the client. Some therapists opt to give them a generic receipt from a receipt book. Others opt to print out a receipt from an accounting software program like Quickbooks. I chose to create my own receipt and then I had Staples turn it into a duplicate receipt pad. I wanted to retain a copy of the exact recipe that I gave the client. This allows me to quickly complete the receipt and put them in a bin until I am ready to complete my billing. If you would like a copy of my receipt form, please visit my website at www.dhaynestherapy.com.

STEP 5:

DURING THE

SESSION

So, you've done the behind-the-scenes work and you're ready to see your first client! How exciting! The very first thing you need to do is breathe. It can be quite nerve-wracking to know that someone is coming to you for help because they feel the problem is totally out of control. That is a daunting responsibility that will dawn on you once you are in session. Never fear, you'll do fine. Just keep things in perspective.

A lot of clients have never gone to a therapist and they really do think that we are magicians that can magically make all their problems disappear. We can't. On top of that, it is not our job to "fix them." I explain therapy to my clients by saying that they are on a journey and they have asked us to help them see the blindspots that they are unable to see. It is a fact that you cannot be and see yourself..unless you use a mirror. We are the mirror for our clients. We go on the journey with them, not to pass judgment, but to allow them to feel safe as they explore their world.

I believe that the act of actively listening is truly a gift to the speaker. Most people don't feel heard or validated for how they feel. You don't have a dog in the fight and you have no prior knowledge so you gain information about who they really are by what they tell you and don't tell you. By listening to what they say and don't say.

Relax. You are the professional and all those years of school as well as those years you spent obtaining your license is about to pay off. Let's begin!

Setting the Mood

Right before the session starts, you need to make the room as comfortable and relaxing as possible. Here are a few things to consider:

- **Music**- Some clients may appreciate calming, soothing music playing in the background. I tend to use Pandora or iHeartRadio during my sessions. I usually turn on classical or relaxation/spa music that do not have any words, but provide a soft and soothing background noise. This is especially helpful if you have officemates within earshot. The music will make it more difficult for them to hear your conversation.

- **White Noise**- I also have a white noise machine. Sometimes some songs or tones may make a person feel saddened. Some people are just more sensitive to sound. Sometimes you may want to listen to something different. If so, a white noise machine works wonders. It sounds like whirling air that is just loud enough to drown out the conversation to others. They are relatively inexpensive depending on how large they are, but they are well worth the expense.

- **Scents**- Some clients find scents to be soothing. Lighting candles or incense can help set the mood of the therapy session. I tend to use a particular incense and my clients say that when they come in and smell it they are almost instantly calmed. Others are sensitive to scents and I make a mental note to not light one during their session.

- **Lighting**- Some clients are more sensitive to light than others or if they are stressed they may have a headache, so having various lighting in the counseling room is important. Usually office buildings have overhead lighting but adding an additional lamp or two can tone the starkness of the room down and create a more soothing atmosphere.

- **Pillows**- Some clients are very tactile and are soothed by rubbing or holding fluffy pillows to them during the session. Having pillows in close proximity provides comfort and a type of protection for some clients.

- **Water**- It's a good idea to keep water around for clients that may cough or need to clear their throat during the session. Having a small fridge helps, but you can keep bottled water around even without a fridge.

- **Candy/Snacks**- I have a candy dish that has the words, "Breathe," on it for my clients that want a "treat" after or even during my session. I only put chocolates in a multitude of flavors in the dish. Most of my clients really enjoy the soothing effect of a Dove chocolate after their session. I don't tend to offer snacks, however, you may decide to provide them for your clients.

- **Tissue**- Make sure you have boxes of tissue readily available for your clients. Some therapists keep in on the couch just in case it's needed. I have a flower stand that is right by the couch and I hand the box to clients as needed.

- **The Room-** Make sure that the overall room is clean and welcoming. Make sure that your carpet or floors are clean, the pillows are fluffed on the chairs and/or couch, and don't have papers laying around especially with client information on it. When your client walks into the room, even if it is your office space and counseling space, they want to feel that you are professional, organized and ready to see them. Clutter and junk is indicative of a cluttered and junky mind. Clients notice everything and they make judgments as to how efficient and effective you are by how organized you are and how smoothly the session flows from beginning to end. So, walk through your office with the eyes of your client to see if there are areas that you need to organize or arrange better prior to their visit.

Additional Paperwork

Even though most of your clients have completed your required forms online or brought them to you the day of your session, you will still need to collect a few pieces of information. The two forms of identification that you will need to obtain are their **driver's license (or picture identification)** and their **insurance card (front and back copy)**. This information will be placed in their client file.

Payment

Yes, we are talking about payment again. You have to decide whether or not you want to accept payment prior to the session or after the session is over. There is no right or wrong way.

Some clients may feel a little miffed with you asking for your payment before they start the session but most do not mind. There are benefits and disadvantages to accepting payment either way. Some things you might want to weigh while making your decision is listed below:

Accepting Payments Prior to the Session

PROS

- You will know for certain that the client is able to pay for the session. When clients go to their doctor's office they usually have to pay their copay or for the entire visit prior to seeing the doctor. Your business can operate the same way.
- If the client is unable to pay, then you can reschedule the session or you can cancel the session. This way you haven't wasted a whole hour that will not be compensated.
- Both of you can focus on the session and when it is over you will be able to move on to the next appointment with ease.

CONS

- The client may feel you are more interested in the payment instead of what is wrong with them.

- Discussions about copays and deductibles will take away from your actual counseling time.

Accepting Payment AFTER the Session

PROS

- The client is able to come in and get started with the session right away.
- The client may feel that you trust them to pay you after the session.

CONS

- You may not get paid for the time you spent with the client.
- Discussing balances, copays, and deductibles after the session may run into the time that you have allotted for another appointment.
- Your next client may be miffed if you did not start your appointment on time.

At the end of the day, it is your business and you can run it any way that you choose to, but I will say that there is nothing worse than a person that appears to be money-hungry or greedy in regards to obtaining money. My suggestion is that you always present a relaxed, business-like demeanor that exudes not only confidence, but warmth. We are working with people. My reason for becoming a mental health therapist (and school counselor) was because I sincerely wanted to help someone. Not so that I could price gauge and run behind my client's money. With that said, we do perform a service and we deserve to be compensated for all the education and certifications we obtained to sit in the "therapist's chair." As therapists we are often imitated by people that have never endured all the obstacles we endured to become therapists. So we can never be duplicated, only imitated. Remember your why, even when collecting money and you'll be on your way to great success!

Ok, I'm off of my soapbox. So let's keeping going.

Diagnostic Evaluation and Goal-Setting

Many therapists have an initial session that can last up to an hour and a half to get all the necessary information completed. This is an in-depth interview to learn more about their familial, educational, spiritual, and vocational history. It is a required form although lengthy. At the end of this document, the therapist and client can discuss which goals need to be established. The question I tend to ask is, *"What do you hope to accomplish and/or change by seeing a therapist?"* They can describe to you how they hope to be once therapy ends. After you create some preliminary goals, because they do change at times, then you can put your preliminary diagnosis down in order to bill insurance.

Some therapists don't complete their diagnostic evaluation during the very first session. I am one of them. I have the clients complete and submit the form to me online so that I can read it prior to the session. Then during the first session, I simply talk with them. My rationale is that I know that many clients have never had therapy before and they are scared and somewhat anxious. I also want to convey to them that I want to hear them out. My last reason is because when I tried to complete the diagnostic during the first session, they were so full of emotions, they would often recount stories and go in-depth when answering a question so the hour would turn into an hour and a half with the majority of the form still left unfinished. So, I made the "executive decision" in my practice to no longer review it the first session, but to do it during the second and even third session if I had a client that needed to be stabilized first. My clients really seem to like being able to fill the long form out at their leisure and then discussing it after some rapport has been established. If you are empathic, which I'm sure you are since you have chosen this field, imagine how it would feel to tell a complete stranger that you have been raped, beaten, attempted suicide, or you have family members that have done those things, during your first time meeting them? You don't even know if you want to come back yet. If you are really traumatized this can really overwhelm you. Even though the diagnostic is definitely a roadmap as to where you are going, I don't believe that skipping a session or two will derail the whole trip.

The Opening Question

Whether you start the first counseling session on the very first visit or after the second visit, you have to have an Opening Question. When I first started my practice, that question bothered me. How do I start? I think that I am a step-by-step type of person and I play out scenarios in my head prior to actually doing what I see. So, I came up with the Opening Question that works for me. Usually, once we are both seated, I will say, *"So, why are we here today?"* or *"What made you pick up the phone to schedule an appointment?"* Even though they mostly book online. I like saying this more than, "How can I help you?" I believe this makes the client feel as if something is really wrong with them. They know that they are there for your help, but I try to make my client's feel that we have a professional relationship and I want to know why we have gathered in this office to talk.

My Opening Question is also very broad. I want to stimulate conversation and make them think. Most clients start off by saying they don't know where to start, but a few know exactly what the issue is and want help dealing with it. Either way, they are talking and soon find that their nervousness has magically disappeared.

Notes or Not

Some therapists take notes and others do not. Some therapists feel that they shouldn't take notes so that the client feels as if they have their undivided attention. Others take the notes to keep up with everything the client says because they don't want to forget. Again the choice is up to you and you have to make the decision based on your attention span. I know that I have a great memory, however, when you are seeing four, five or even eight clients back- to- back those clients turn into hours of serious concentrating and that can be very tiring. I take notes to keep me focused as well as to keep up with keywords that a client says. I don't write full sentences on my notepad. I jot down major points that will trigger my memory. You may opt to write sentences, but that is too time consuming in my opinion.

This is an area where you have to go with your gut instinct. If I notice a "suspicious" client stop talking every time I start writing then I may stop writing or I will address the issue by assuring him or her that my notes are for me alone and they are confidential. I never want a client to feel that I'm more interested in getting what they say down more than I am interested in them as a person. I do people work in session and paperwork out of session and I do my best to make sure my clients not only hear me say that but they see it in my actions. This is why I do quick key words and then make eye contact with the client to ensure that I am focused once again on them. As you get more familiar with your client and with sitting in the therapist's chair, multitasking will become easier.

Recording Sessions

Some therapists like to record their sessions. Most will use a voice recorder while others will use a video camera to record their clients. Using these techniques instead of writing down notes is an option, but you must get written permission from the client prior to recording them. Personally, I feel as if recording what they say can be somewhat evasive and off-putting.

In this age of technology, we have to be extremely careful with how we store client information. So, if you opt to use these methods to record sessions please use extreme caution.

The TV Therapist versus The Real Therapist

On television most therapists are portrayed as a man or woman that sits in a big chair, looks up and you and down at their notes, and says "uh huh" or "How did that make you feel?" over and over ad nauseum! This couldn't be further from the truth...I hope! However, some clients really think that is how therapists behave. Like they are a specimen that we are examining until we make our diagnosis and deem the crazy. NOT!

Self-Disclosure

Some therapists subscribe to a specific theory and if the theory says that is how they are supposed to behave...being the watcher... they will do it. I'm more of a realist. I get in the trenches with my clients. I'm not so emotionally attached that I cry when they cry, but I definitely allow myself to be in the moment with them. They are not specimens, but people and I am a person as well. The only difference is that I'm a professional person and it is my job to shoulder their pain so they feel safe enough to explore it while in session. To me that takes conversation...with boundaries. Some therapists get so caught up that they "over share" and the client can feel as if they are the therapists and the therapist is the client! That is a big NO-NO! They are not paying you to listen to you discuss your divorce and grief.

They came to you for help. So, some self disclosure can be helpful but it has to be very limited so that the professional relationship is not compromised.

Counselor - Client Boundaries

That brings me to clients that begin to believe you are their friend. Yes, you are their friend because you want them to trust you enough to talk to you without judgment, but you are still a professional. We all know about conflicts of interest and the severe repercussions that come about when counselor-client relationships become a little too close for comfort. So it is a delicate balance between being a "type of friend" and yet keeping a comfortable distance. Sometimes it takes having a conversation about the "boundaries" that must stay very clear at all times. If boundaries continue to be overstepped then you may have to discontinue your "counseling relationship" and refer the client to another therapist,

Some signs that the Counselor-Client relationship boundaries have been breached are:

- ✓ They call you anytime, day or night, as if they are chatting with a dear friend and not to discuss a scheduling or counseling issues.
- ✓ They call you anytime day or night.
- ✓ They drop-in at your office to say hi or to ask you a question.
- ✓ They feel that they should have special privileges such as extended sessions.

✓ They ask you personal questions during your sessions.

✓ They flirt with you.

✓ They make sexual advances toward you.

If these or other situations occur that make you feel uneasy, please contact your counseling mentor or colleague. Then act on it swiftly by addressing the situation directly.

Ending the Session

At the five or ten minute mark of the session, I will inform the client that we have five or ten minutes more so I will either begin to discuss what I hope we are able to begin working on during or next session or I will ask them if they have any final thoughts. Most clients respect the time limit, but some clients will attempt to squeeze out a couple more minutes with you by bringing up a big emotion topic. I will usually state that I believe that is a very heavy subject and that we should save that until next time in addition to the fact that I have another client waiting. Now, at times, I have listened if they sincerely have reached a major aha moment and/or if I know that I don't have any more clients after this client finishes. However, I will not let a session go on and on. Since I have already warned them about five or ten minutes prior to the end of their session, I will only allot five to ten more minutes of overtime. Anything more and we are getting into an extended counseling session that will be billed.

After we complete the session and I have collected payment, I will give them a receipt. Prior to moving to an online appointment scheduler, we used to use some of this time to figure out when they wanted to schedule another appointment. A counseling session is usually one hour with 50 minutes being allotted for actual counseling time and the last 10 minutes being allotted for billing and scheduling, but this often turned into 15 minutes of scheduling. With my online appointment scheduler, I have cut out that step. I accept payment, give them a receipt and they are done for the day. They can then schedule their next appointment with me on their phone or on a computer at their leisure. I use SimplePractice and I think it is a fantastic tool on so many levels but more on that in the next session.

Once the client walks out with their receipt in hand you are finished. You did it! Your first private therapy session is over and you are official! Congratulations! Isn't this fun?! I was so nervous prior to my first session but once I completed it I was hooked! I hope that you are feeling the same way.

STEP 6:

AFTER THE

SESSION

So, you survived your first session! Again, congratulations! Now the hard work really begins.

Paperwork

You've probably heard about the massive amount of paperwork that is created while running your private practice. There is some truth to this, however, if you stay on top of your paperwork then it is not as daunting as it seems.

When I started out, I had no idea about what they meant by "paperwork." I knew that the application process to insurance panels was lengthy, but what could be so hard about writing down a couple of notes. Well, I learned quickly.

As a private therapist, much of your paperwork will consist of filing notes and receipts, entering notes into a cloud based storage program, billing insurance, and possibly completing short term disability forms or preparing your forms for legal documents. Each of these tasks take time to complete. However, the more you do them the faster you will complete them.

Session Notes

Some therapists opt to write notes during their session and then to simply file these notes away in a secure file cabinet. This was the standard practice until everything became cloud based. Now, even therapists that write notes during the session will flesh them out in a cloud based system after the session.

I used to use the system, Genbook, to schedule appointments and to store client notes. Due to rising costs, I chose to switch to SimplePractice. SimplePractice allows my clients to create a profile and book their own appointment. After the session, I am able to log-in and go into the notes section to enter my treatment plan, session notes, and any psychotherapy notes (private) as well as to bill or pay out the client's invoice. Due to these features as well as the pricing, I have used them for several years now and they keep getting better and better.

Whether you use paper or cloud-based systems is not really important until you are asked to present this information to an attorney or to an insurance company for a disability claim. At that time, you will have to copy your handwritten notes, which honestly doesn't look to professional or you can print them off from the cloud-based system. Do you see why I chose the latter? In actuality, I keep written and typed in notes, but it is so much easier to print the fully fleshed out notes from a cloud-based system.

Systems

Systems is a very important word when discussing paperwork. You have to have a system or way that you complete and organize your work. As you create your office systems, imagine having to teach what you do to a new employee. It needs to be concise and produce the same results if each of the steps are completed the same way each time. Same steps produce the same results.

Standard Operating Procedure (SOP)

If you think about it, most corporations and organizations have a Standard Operating Procedure (SOP) Manual for their business. This is a step-by-step document that will teach new employees or remind the old employees as to what you would have them do. This book is a life-saver so that you don't have to continuously repeat yourself to new employees. Some CEOs have opted to create an online document in Google Docs that allows the new employee to not only read the document, but add steps to help others understand how they do what they do. They have to sign a contract that the information included in the SOP is the owners, but it is a great way to continually update and expanded what a person does day to day on their job.

So as you piece together your business and how you like it to be operate on a daily basis, it would be a great idea to create your own SOP. Not only will it be a great guide for a new employee but you can review it so see how you can get your business to run more efficiently over time. I know that the way that I ran my business when I first started is not the way that I currently run my business now. Some things are similar but I strive to make it more streamlined, reduce the number of steps, and to get more done in less time more efficiently.

Is it sinking in that you are an entrepreneur yet? Yes, you are and the business side is great because it ensures that your business continues to grow and make money. However, there are parts of it that can make you uncomfortable but that is one of the growing pains of being the boss.

Filing Systems

When you have a practice, keeping records in order and updated is very important. Client information can change at any time so you need to be able to pull their folder or pull up their information to update their file quickly.

Even if you use a cloud-based system to enter your notes and other client information, you will need to have another filing system. All you need are secure filing cabinets. What you put into the filing cabinets and how you put things into the filing cabinet is what really matters.

Client Profile Information

Remember the documents that you requested from your client prior to the session? Now you need to put the copy of their driver's license, insurance card, and any other paper documents they brought to you into the client's file. I chose to color code my files. I use purple folders for payment information and manila folders for handwritten notes and other papers I receive concerning the clients. I started out separating these folders by color in two filing cabinets, but I have since began to store them together, side by side. Initially, I thought that I would store them as a notes side and a billing side, but after having to look for information in both folders, it became easier for me to simply grab both folders in one fell swoop. Efficiency!

Purple Folders

In the purple folder, I include their insurance card copy and my duplicate of the receipt that I gave to them. I also have a sheet that I created a client documentation sheet that includes information such as their name, date of birth, address as well as the date I saw them, and the date I billed their insurance company. To purchase and download a copy of this form, please visit my website at www.dhaynestherapy.com.

Manila Folders

In the manila folder, I include my handwritten notes, paper forms that they downloaded and completed by hand, and legal or disability requests. If you would like a copy of the folder check-off sheet that I use to ensure that I have all documentation, in paper form or online, then please visit my website at www.dhaynestherapy.com.

Client Numbers

On each of my folders, I have the client's first and last name. However, some businesses opt to put an initial and last name or they use a client number instead of their name. I do assign each of my clients a client number because it is required by most insurance companies. You can start with 001, but I opted to start with 200, just to look professional. However, the client number or number system is up to you. Just make sure that you keep track of it and keep it in a secure place.

Billing Insurance

Now for the part we have all been waiting for...the pies de resistance! Money! There is nothing wrong with acknowledging that you love what you do and that you do want to be paid well for your services. That is being honest because even though I love it and have done it for free on occasion, I still have bills to pay and the desire to have a good life. So in order to do that, I have to be compensated and you need to be compensated as well.

I took time out to say this because there are some that are quite money-hungry and will try to get all the money. Greed is unattractive and makes me wonder about a person's motives. Are you here to help people or simply make money? That is a question everyone should answer not out loud because you may not say the politically correct thing, but what's in your heart. Your business will show you what you really feel in your heart. Either your clients will love you and work with you, since you are human too, or they will flee after one or two sessions because they don't feel heard or maybe they feel judged. So, this is a very serious question that needs to be answered prior to seeing clients.

So, with that said, hopefully your business will flourish and you will have lots and lots of billing to do. Besides, that is a good problem to have! Therapists deal with this problem in different ways. Some don't want the hassle of billing so they hire an outside company to bill for them. Most of these billing companies will require that you send them billing information on each of your clients as well as your log-ins to all the insurance agencies your clients belong to. Pretty scary, huh? It is so you have to make sure whoever you are sending this confidential information to is legitimately a business. A contract depicting how much they will get once they bill for you should be negotiated. Once all of that is in place, you will simply fax to them the names of the people you saw that week and they will do the rest. Many have forms you complete first and you fax the client roster on that sheet.

This is a good resource if you are really short on time and/or don't like to worry about such matters. Just know that they are getting a fee for their services once you receive the money. They can also act as a collection agency if the client chooses not to pay. This alleviates you from being the "bad guy" and they would talk directly with your collection/billing company instead of you.

Other therapists, like myself, want to know how their business works inside and out. We are the ones that tackle billing by ourselves. Let me be clear, once the client information is entered it is a relatively quick and easy process to bill that client, but the billing issues can be hell on earth! Calling insurance agencies, being on hold, being passed from one person to another and back again with no clear answers can be a big headache! I have said some "choice" words many a times as I was transferred yet again for the fourth or fifth time. It is incredibly frustrating and yet I wouldn't change it for the world.

Those frustrating situations happen every so often and you learn to roll with the punches. Insurance agencies including Medicaid will sometimes pay without hesitation, but if the client makes any change to their plan it can throw the well-oiled machine into a tail spin. Once you accept that this will happen from time to time, when it does happen it is not a shock, but part of what it takes to have your own business.

Electronic Billing

So, when the well-oiled machine is working properly, billing your client is easy. Since you are an approved provider, you should have received information to access their websites to submit your claims. Simply log in and put your information into the shaded fields and submit. It's really that easy. Once you do it once, the computer systems generally save your client and business information so you can quickly submit those pages.

You will have to re-enter billing information because some of it changes. Some of the fields you will have to enter information into each time you bill are as follows:

CPT Codes

CPT codes stand for Current Procedural Terminology. It is a medical code that is used to report medical, surgical, and diagnostic procedures and services to entities such as physicians, health insurance companies and accreditation organizations. Therapists use it to report diagnostic procedures to the insurance company. A sample CPT code that is used frequently in therapeutic billing is **90837**. This number means that the client was seen in a therapeutic office for one hour. Another CPT code frequently used is **90791** which means that the session was for a diagnostic evaluation. This code tends to pay more because insurance companies understand that this session may last for a longer period of time. It can usually only be used once.

To find out more about CPT codes, review the literature that your receive from each insurance company you are approved to provide services for or visit https://www.ama-assn.org/practice-management/cpt for more information.

Once you learn your basic codes, you will continue to reuse those codes over and over. If you would like a CPT code cheat sheet, purchase and download my Fee Schedule Form from my website at www.dhaynestherapy.com.

ICD-10 Codes

Guess what? It's time for you to diagnose! It's going to feel strange at first because one can't help, but think that you aren't a medical doctor. However, you are a medical provider so you will have to diagnose mental disorders just as a doctor diagnoses medical disorders. This fact is scary and exciting. What you diagnose a person with will not only stay with them mentally, but on formal documents that could affect whether or not they get disability or employed at a job. My advice is to take this part very seriously.

When I first started we were using the ICD-9 and many of us simply stated that the client had an Adjustment Disorder, Unspecified until we gained more information. Simple right? Well, after the DSM-5 was born, most insurance agencies decided they didn't like that "non-diagnosis." That is understandable, but it is hard to pinpoint a diagnosis after one hour of meeting someone. I have had clients to come in stating they had gender dysphoria only to figure out in session five that they are schizophrenic as well.

So, in order for you get compensated by insurance companies for the hour of work you already completed, you have to give them a tentative diagnosis. So, I tend to diagnose them with their presenting problem (depression or anxiety), the first session and then change the diagnosis once I have more information to go on such as PTSD, Bipolar Disorder, or Borderline Personality Disorder. Thank goodness for the handy dandy DSM-5 for the guidelines to follow in order to make as accurate a diagnosis as possible.

Once you have chosen your diagnosis from the DSM-5, you will enter the ICD-10 code for that disorder. The ICD-10 is The International Classification of Diseases, Tenth Edition (**ICD-10**) is a clinical cataloging system. The ICD-10 code generally starts with an F and then a number. For instance, the ICD-10 code for depression is F33.0. Some insurance agencies will have you type in the dot and others will want the number to look like F330. It's the same thing just the preference of the company's billing system.

DHCS TIP: You will probably end up being a provider on several insurance panels. You will need some type of system in place to keep up with all the log-in information. Keeping the website address, your username, password, and contact information in several locations is a great idea. Most therapists keep them in the notes or contact section of their cell phone, in a notebook or password booklet in a locked location, and/or on a document. Saving this information in multiple locations (and updating the log-in regularly) will be a tremendous saver of time and effort when you are billing insurance companies.

Unpaid Accounts

What happens when everything is working like a well-oiled machine and then you hit a snafu? A client said that they had insurance but the insurance has been canceled and refuses to reimburse you. Or what if the client sits through the whole session and at the end, tells you that they are unable to pay until a couple of days from that particular date? What if you bill the insurance and there is still a portion that the client has to pay to meet?

Don't despair. More times than not, a client will readily pay for the session if there is a problem. Be prepared. Some clients may not return until they have met their deductible, but others will continue to see you until their deductible is met.

For those difficult clients, you have a couple of options. They are as follows:

1. You can opt to hire a billing service to take care of your insurance billing and they will act as a collection agency to attempt to collect your money.

2. You can contact your client via phone, e-mail, text and mail to ask for your money. You may have to continue to call, text or email them to respond and pay you. I usually start with a phone call or text, then I try an e-mail, and finally I send a formal delinquency letter. The letters start "friendly" and each month become more "stern." To purchase and download a copy of my delinquency letter, please visit my website at www.dhaynestherapy.com.

3. Quite frankly, you may end up with an unpaid bill in your files. If you haven't hired a collection agency then you may have to eat that deficit. Now, of course, you will discontinue treating that client until the balance is paid, but you can also deduct that loss off of your taxes. I know. It's not the best case scenario, but every single business out there takes a loss at times. So, even though these

instances are uncommon, they do exist and I want you to be mentally

prepared for it.

BLINDSPOTS

We have covered several sections that have hopefully provided some insider tips to people that are considering becoming a private therapist or who are already licensed therapists seeking open their own private practice. The Blindspots chapter will examine grey areas that are not usually discussed in one cohesive format.

Compassion Fatigue

Most therapists that choose to open a private practice or who serve clients through an organization do so because they love the work. They love the feeling that comes when you know you have helped someone through a dark time and they are stabilized enough to walk alone without your assistance for awhile. I tell my clients that my goal is to work myself out of a job. It is not necessary for clients to see you for the rest of their life. The ultimate goal is for them to identify their triggers or what is hindering them and then find ways to cope with or overcome the problem. It's that simple. So when you achieve that it is a special feeling.

With that said, it is an awesome responsibility to shoulder the pain, trauma, and secrets of all of your clients day after day. Add to that the reality that you are a person and that you have your own issues and problems. Clients are paying you to not worry about your own problems and to join them in their pain and/or sorrow. So, we often push aside our own issues and pain until we can no longer ignore the fact that we need help as well.

Self-care is of the utmost importance for mental health therapists but it is the part we often forget about. Compassion Fatigue is the burnout that therapists sometimes feel when they have been caretaking for so long that they lose the compassion for their clients and they forget about taking care of themselves. It is similar to what takes place in hospitals when we see doctors and nurses that have become desensitized to gory and bloody injuries. They get hyperfocused on the injury and the steps to help the injured person that they often push down their ability to nurture the person with the injury. This is what some people refer to when they say that the doctor or nurse does not have good "bedside manners," which means they have no empathy for the person they are treating and the patient feels that. When a therapist begins to feel that way their clients feel it. You will come off as robotic because you are doing what you are "supposed to do," but the joy and true empathic emotion behind it has been lost. This is why it is so important to take care of yourself and to schedule breaks from your job.

Some ways to detach from your job and use self-care to prevent compassion fatigue or burnout are as follows:

1. **Mental Breaks-** Schedule mental breaks throughout the day. Whether you turn off your phone and sit in quiet, meditate, take a class at a local gym, or take a nap, make sure you carve out some time for yourself.

2. **Vacations**- Make sure you schedule time away from the office. Take a day or two to not do any work. Ride to the beach, mountains, or visit great friends and family to rejuvenate yourself. Connecting to nature goes a long way to rejuvenate yourself.

3. **Write**- As much as we tell our clients to write down their thoughts and feelings, we often forget that we can write down what we feel and think as well. Journaling about our day-to-day experiences really helps to alleviate the daily stress that we are under. Considering the fact that our experiences with our clients are confidential, you can't always talk about what you experienced with anyone. However, you can write about it and as long as you don't include names that could identify your client, you should be fine. If you are interested in purchasing a journal for therapists, please visit my website www.dhaynestherapy.com to purchase my journal entitled, *The Vault: For Therapists.* It is a great tool to store your thoughts and feelings throughout the year.

4. **Talk to Someone**- My professors used to say that, "Therapists should have a therapist." This is an absolute fact! Everyone could use someone to talk to that provides that objective listening ear. Therapists are no different. We take in a lot and in order to not become overloaded it is important to release those things that bother us in our personal and professional lives. If you don't feel comfortable

speaking to a therapist (go figure) then make sure you have a supportive group of friends you can talk with when you are feeling burdened. I will often call my friends and tell them that I need their energy. They already know that means that I had a heavy session. Sometimes I will mention what really is bothering me and other times I choose not to talk about it and choose to laugh and talk about anything other than what occurred during those sessions. Either way they understand me and give me the space to breathe and regroup.

Find out what brings you joy and peace and then do that. You and your clients will be glad you did.

Branding

Branding is essentially the things that you do to make your business stand out from the rest and encompasses various elements. I could write an entire book on branding, but for the purposes of this book, I'm going to introduce a few elements that you should consider if you are interested in branding your business.

Logo - Most therapists create and/or purchase a logo that represents their business. When I got started in business, I didn't think about having a logo, but as I learned more and more about the business side of the business I decided to have a logo created to represent my business.

When I began to think about a logo, the McDonald's symbol immediately came to mind. Those golden arches are known worldwide and even babies can recognize those McDonald's arches and understand that french fries are at that place. I didn't expect my logo to be world renown, but I did feel that it would help set me apart from the other therapists in town.

I sat down and brainstormed what I wanted my logo to represent. I knew that I wanted my business name tied into the logo and then I wanted the actual symbol to mean something. I came up with puzzle pieces and used the tagline, the missing piece. That worked for awhile until I had a couple people tell me that my logo reminded them of the autism logo. When I looked it up, it did remind me of it even though the only things it had in common with mine was that it did look like puzzle pieces and there was a puzzle piece missing. Who knew?! So, the $30 logo I had created by Staples had to be changed.

I decided to get it professionally done this time as well as to update my website. The logo ended up including my name, but I wanted a butterfly to be included in the logo. I didn't want it to be too girly since I see men and women at my practice and I wanted it to include my favorite color, blue. Lastly, I wanted it to be almost like an optical illusion. I wanted you to see it as a butterfly, but then see something else if you looked closer. A small order. I know. However, my logo developer worked his magic and came up with the blue butterfly whose wings are a man and woman looking at each other. I loved it! Best of all it is mine!

So, as you think about branding your business logo you need to consider the following:

1. **Business Colors**- What colors best represent your business or yourself? Research what colors actually mean and how they affect others that are viewing them. I wanted my colors to be soothing and calming. You may like vibrant, rich colors that represent your personality. The choice is yours.

2. **Symbols**- What symbol best represents you and your business? I often see pictures of families, trees, and hands that represent either the person's target market or suggest how they plan to help their clients. This is important because you will be amazed at what draws a person to your business. I have had some say they chose me because they love the color blue, like my butterfly or just liked the set-up of my website. Either way, it is important that you pay attention to detail because your clients are definitely looking.

Business Cards- You will need to purchase some business cards. If you do not have a logo then some therapists opt to use a picture of themselves. They are still branding their business but they are the brand instead of a symbol representing their brand. Either tactic works and is up to your personal preference.

You will use your business cards to ensure that people can find you in case they have questions or would like to make an appointment with you.

You can leave your business cards at establishments or leave them with people at speaking engagements in case they want to book an appointment or speak with you further.

My first set of business cards came from Staples, they were plain and not even glossy. As my practice grew, I purchased new, fancy business cards. So the key is to simply start. How you start your business is not permanent. As it matures, so will your content and products. All you have to do is ensure that it is professional and available in case you need them and you will need them.

Social Media Presence

In the age of technology having a social media presence is mandatory especially when you are trying to build a brand. Facebook and Instagram provide FREE business pages so that you can advertise your business. They are great tools to use to create a buzz about your business. If you add videos of yourself, this allows your audience to get to know you even more as they decide whether they want to take you on as their therapist.

Twitter, Periscope, YouTube, even SnapChat are other awesome ways to advertise your business. These entities allow you to briefly jump on and connect with your audience. Whether you are all business and you like to teach about various subjects or you're funny and creative, these sites allow you to build your brand and to capture your audience long before they become paying clients.

Email Marketing

E-mail marketing has become another staple that can assist you in developing your brand. Constant Contact as well as MailChimp are awesome ways to reach your current clients as well as to attract new ones. You can have people fill in their e-mail address to visit your website or you can find other creative ways to get people's e-mail address. Once you have their address then you can create newsletters and/or offers that will drive them to your business or at the least keep them updated as to current events within your practice.

Webinars, Courses and Conferences

You can also build your brand with webinars, courses, and conferences. You can create online webinars in which you will video yourself teaching a particular subject that your clients will pay to view. Webinars are taped as the therapist is teaching other live people. Then that video is sold to other people that missed the live presentation.

Courses are similar, but they tend to have more of a classroom feel and you often will not be videoed as a part of the actual course material. Courses may include a PowerPoint presentation with an included voiceover. Slides and video may be included in the course. Usually a test is given at the end and continuing education credits are awarded for completing the course.

Conferences can be created to address a particular need on a larger scale. Participants will sign up and pay to attend the conference. Usually several speakers will address the audience at the conference. The conference can last one day up to a whole week. Conferences can also be videotaped and then purchased by participants that were unable to attend.

Marketability

The name of the Branding game is to make yourself as marketable as possible. You want people to come see you or buy your products because they like what you offer. Branding yourself should make people feel that if they visit you, then they will have their specific problem solved because you are the expert in that area.

Honestly no one really is an expert because there is always more to learn but if you have honed your craft and you are always striving to learn all that you can, especially in your specialty area, then you will become a recognized expert in that field.

Certifications- We already talked about having an area of specialty, but you can continue to add to your certifications. Certifications are those areas of specialty that you have excelled at and you will have the letters behind your name to showcase these areas of expertise. Some possible certifications that you can pursue that will build your brand and expertise are as follows:

National Certified Counselor (NCC)- This credential tells the world that you are nationally recognized as one of the top mental health counselors. There are strict guidelines that will qualify you and there are yearly fees to keep this credential.

Distance Credentialed Counselor (DCC)- This is a new credential and it certifies that you have been certified to provide counseling via telephone, video, and e-mail. This is great because it opens your doors to anyone located in the state or states that you have licensure. Unfortunately, it does not open the door wide enough, at this time, for you to counsel and bill clients around the world. There is a yearly fee for this licensure.

Licensed Professional Supervisor (LPCS)- Once you have had your license for two years, you can apply to become a Licensed Professional Counselor Supervisor. This license allows you to bring new therapists in the field. The process is two years and you can charge your LPCIs for your services. There is also a fee due every two years and continuing education requirements needed to continue to keep this license up-to-date.

In closing, I hope that this book has been and will continue to be a great resource as you build your mental health practice. It has been my honor to pour everything that I have learned, that I didn't know I needed to know, along the years into this book.

Please take a moment to send me feedback on what you liked about this book and any other pertinent information that you would like to see in future books. You can email me at dhaynes@dhaynestherapy.com.

I thank you for your purchase and I pray that this book makes your journey into the mental health field as easy as possible.

References

Application Information
**Check with your local Labor and Licensing Board for more information.

Business EIN/Tax ID number
https://sa.www4.irs.gov/modiein/individual/index.jsp

Forms Information
Visit www.dhaynestherapy.com to purchase and download forms.

Healthcare Providers Service Organization (HPSO)- Malpractice Insurance
159 E. County Line Road
Hatboro, PA 19040-1218

Professional Liability Phone: 1-800-982-9491
Personal Insurance Phone: 1-877-215-2311
Fax for Applications: 1-800-739-8818
Fax for Correspondence: 1-800-758-3635

Insurance companies listings
Visit www.dhaynestherapy.com to download forms.

Licensure Information
http://www.cce-global.org/BusinessLicensureServices/StateLicensure
Center for Credentialing & Education, Inc.
3 Terrace Way, Suite B
Greensboro, NC 27403-3660
Phone: (888) 817-8283 (toll free)
Fax: (336) 482-2852
E-Mail: cce@cce-global.org
Internet: www.cce-global.org

National Provider Identification Number
https://nppes.cms.hhs.gov/NPPES/Welcome.do

NPI customer service: **800.465.3203** | 800.692.2326 (TTY) | customerservice@npienumerator.com

Testing Information
National Board for Certified Counselors   www.nbcc.org

Made in the USA
Middletown, DE
08 August 2017